# SUNSETS AND STARS

## Hibbah Haddam

Copyright © 2021 Hibbah Haddam

ISBN: 978-1-7376447-0-5
ISBN: 978-1-7376447-1-2 (ebook)

Printed in the United States of America

*to mani, my maternal grandmother*
*may God have mercy on your soul.*
*to my maternal grandfather-*
*a natural storyteller, may you always find peace*
*and love.*
*to my paternal grandparents-*
*may God have mercy on your souls.*
*your loved ones continue to learn*
*and be inspired by you.*

*enjoy the sweetness of a date; enjoy the last fiber attached to its solid pit. watch the setting of the sun to remind you that endings are inevitable.*

*and lastly, look up at the stars: everlasting symbols of hope in the middle of the darkness.*

# CONTENTS

I.
a conversation

gravity
concrete sunrises
sometimes she
date pits and sunsets and stars
sun's kisses
love is
remarkable human mind

II.
unwelcomed visitor
don't fret little nightbird
a displaced dream
graffiti
birthdays
losing my voice

III.
to a loved one
to the people of great sorrow
the basics
words
eman
healing
love left behind

# I.

*"The world is full of obvious things which
nobody by any chance ever observes."*

-ARTHUR CONAN DOYLE,

THE HOUND OF BASKERVILLES

## *a conversation*

what if I told you
that the one thing I wish for the most was
a conversation

words spoken face to face,
stories not written or told
through the lens of someone else,
but directly from the source.

I yearn
for that conversation.
all I have now
are pictures
passed down stories
and imagination.

*gravity*

your rough edges
had no effect
on the kind soul reflected
in your brown eyes
I see

your smile
radiating warmth
the brightness of a
setting sun
powerful I know

your gravity
                pulling me
                                down
                                        down
            falling freely,
                        gently.

## concrete sunrises

the early morning sun's reflection on glass
chases me as I run past.

it begs me for an embrace
or just a simple glance.

a moment to
            pause
                  in the middle of the rush.

for it knows the power it holds
to turn humdrum feelings
into gold.
                  to shine the light
              that would inspire
            the words I write
          on this paper.

## sometimes she

sometimes she
flies to the moon
with a Sinatra flare

sometimes she
feels good and
proclaims it to the world
like Nina before her

sometimes she
yearns for a Sunday kind of love
like an Etta tune

sometimes she
wishes she could forget you
as easily as a gust of wind
and with an Abdelhalim melody

sometimes she
needs a reminder from El Harrachi
that no matter where she travels
she can always return home

sometimes she
sings along with the star of the East
and dances with Motown gems
sometimes—

but always

with soul

## *date pits and sunsets and stars*

dates taste sweeter
when shared
from one platter
pit of my stomach
where the warmth of a laugh goes

sunsets shine brighter
when shared
star in the sky
is the place where my dreams
at night reside.

## *sun's kisses*

lift your head high
and see
specks of gold on green

the sun's kisses on trees
and on you and on me

## *love is*

love is stronger
than hate

love is pure,
much more than
a simple emotion.

love is finding your passion,
working on your craft
no matter the situation.

love is strength,
aiding us in the process of
conquering our darkness.

love has always been inquired upon,
dissected and studied,
for as long as hearts
began beating in human shells.

love is heavy,
four letters in the English dictionary
carrying so much weight;
love is an action—

love is love,
as certain and real
as death.

## *remarkable human mind*

a gift and a curse it seems:
our ability to reflect
on past mistakes.

a gift and a curse it seems:
our ability to repeat
those same mistakes
over and over—
the remarkable human mind.

# II.

*"Those who dream by day are cognizant of many things which escape those who dream only by night."*

-EDGAR ALLAN POE, ELEONORA

*"Deep into that darkness peering, long I stood there, wondering, fearing, doubting, dreaming dreams no mortal ever dared to dream before."*

-EDGAR ALLAN POE, THE RAVEN

## unwelcomed visitor

my friend,
I knew I could count on you.

honoring me with your presence,
you visit once again.
at times when all I want to do
is forget,

forget,
not reflect,
turning on every brain cell in my
exhausted overspent overthinking
mind, forget
not remember,
every aching wound in my body
my soul, forget
every negative thought
pulsing, unable to stop
thinking the worst,
forget.

I plead,
insomnia, let me be
for what keeps me going through the day
is the chance to shut off all the noises,
the voices occupying spaces
in my head at night.

## *don't fret, little nightbird*

spending its days in silence
and its nights in song

releasing all emotions
the nightbird sings

the nightbird sings
a tune from a burdened soul

the nightbird sings
until its soul rests

the nightbird sings
until there's no reason to sing

a reason to sing
no more

## *a displaced dream*

enclosed in an old dream
lies a garden far
from reality's grasp

enclosed in a faded silver locket
lies a picture
encapsulating a story
of pain and hope

enclosed in this weathered music box
lies a tune
reawakening the spirits
of once lived moments

enclosed in these
bullet
     ridden
clay
     colored
house
     walls

               lies a courtyard
               diffusing scents
               of rose and jasmine

enclosed in my aged rib cage
lies a heart
yearning for the love of you
          "ya baladi" *

how remarkable is it
that far from reality's grasp
one could enclose a garden
in a new dream

*oh, my country

*graffiti*

permanence
perhaps feelings
of nostalgia
a firm expression

                    I was here

*birthdays*

it was one year ago
      today

the sun shone and
my lungs were filled with
a Mediterranean breeze

strong blue waves were
crashing against boulders
as I
breathed in
        and out

for a moment
all was peaceful
all was calm

it was one year ago
      today

we sat together
and celebrated your
78 years of life

it is one year now
gray skies are what I see
but just as waves
      recede

and return

so shall the sun

## losing my voice

it's the "m" in "my name is"
or the "s" in "stop"

the "a" in absolutely
or the "l" in "love"

it's the fear of being stuck
unable to find the words
to complete the verse
the mind knows by heart

pebble by pebble
I have removed these stones
letting the stream flow
knowing with certainty that they will
     return:
the dreaded moment of a stutter

I remove these stones
knowing they will return
trusting in Him and
believing in the very voice
that escapes these lips

# III.

*"Happiness can be found even in the darkest of times, if one only remembers to turn on the light."*

-J.K. ROWLING,

HARRY POTTER AND THE PRISONER OF AZKABAN

*"After all this time?" "Always."*

-J.K. ROWLING,

HARRY POTTER AND THE DEATHLY HALLOWS

## *to a loved one*

may the sky above you
remain blue and clear

may the breeze that blows your way
be gentle and kind
cooling you from any fires
you've been forced to enter
as Abraham faced before.

may the sun shine and light your way
and when darkness falls
may the stars glow
and the moon give you comfort

and when monsters intimidate you
to stay in bed
may God bless you with the strength
to wake up
and continue.

## *to the people of great sorrow*

historical wrongs
may have led you down a path
of great sorrow,
but I can't seem to fathom
nor understand
your ability to push back
and grow.

is it in the sacrifice?
unable to pursue your own
dreams and desires
do you recycle the remnants
for others?

tell me,
when you turn your sorrow
into beautiful music
are you weeping as well?

or are you too busy
creating, moving
like you were born to do?

*the basics*

stay still,
my anxious heart
your rapid beating
making it harder for oxygen to reach
the depths of my starving lungs.

so we retreat,
making our way towards the base of a living
    tree,
to find solace in the traditions held by those
    before us.

we place our worn palms
against the rough coat of a trunk
a human pulse
sending invisible vibrations through the
    thick layers of bark.

tree branches embracing us warmly,
warm roots keeping us grounded.
the intricate design of leaves
forcing us to look upward and trace
                the movement of a single bird's
    pair of
                wings.

oh heart of mine,
it is with this I remind you,

you can fly.

so, stay still
my anxious heart,
and let these lungs be full and content
as they are meant to be.

## *words*

five letters full of meaning?
or just a pretext
as Rumi proclaimed before

the first thing a baby says
or something many yearn to hear

words could be powerful
with the ability to move
the hearts of a nation or a people

but are they enough to spur action?

for some
words are revealed out of a tangled web
out of a twisted tongue
but for some
they flow naturally
like water from a cool spring

words can fill a page with nonsense
or knowledge
a beauty so sweet

we read books with words
that help us imagine
and paint a picture
in our hearts and minds

and maybe
just maybe
hold the spark to light
this soul's revolution

*eman*

faith is
a constant state of learning
how to seek the moon
behind a cover of clouds

## *healing*

I sink my feet in cool waters
healing neglected wounds
as I call out

to all the places I call home
to predictable routines
and the warmth of the sun on my skin
to the sounds and conversations my ears
  have taken in
to the beauty He has graciously sprinkled all
  around me
to all the unfamiliar particles I have breathed
  in

all reminding me of something familiar

## *love left behind*

I close my eyes and
I see you

I see you
in the kindness of a stranger,
in the wisdom of an elder,
in every genuine smile.

I close my eyes and
I find you

I find you
in the sweetness of flowers,
in the healing powers of herbs.

I open my eyes and
I see you

in my eyes is a reflection
of the love you left behind and
like a seed,
it grows.

❋ ❋ ❋

# ACKNOWLEDGEMENT

a big thank you to anyone who has read through this collection in its entirety (you're awesome). if you have made it this far and enjoyed my work, I kindly ask that you leave me a **book review** on Amazon (which would make you *super* awesome)

a second big thank you to my family and friends for their continuous support and encouragement, and to my English teachers in the past for their knowledge and encouragement

Editor:
Nicole Fegan

Cover photography by:
Idina Risk
(pexels.com)

Back Cover photography by:
Rakicevic Nenad
(pexels.com)

# ABOUT THE AUTHOR

## Hibbah Haddam

Hibbah Haddam, aka a woman with many nicknames, grew up in the Washington D.C. metro area. She has a background in biology and while science is her second love, writing has always been her first. She began writing poetry, prose, and short stories at a young age. She draws inspiration from her faith, her love of nature, and her general curiosity of the inner and outer workings of the human spirit (she's a people watcher for sure). When she's not learning new skills and writing, she is trying to figure out the shortest way to explain to people what she does for a living. sunsets and stars is her first published collection.

You can follow her adventures on Instagram @thesilverteapotjournal or online at silverteapotjournal.com.